Dedication

This series is written in the loving memory of a gracious boy gone too soon. Kaine Micheal Neal had a way of bringing a smile to anyone's face; a sense of empathy, gratitude and wisdom that needn't be carried by one so young. May we all aspire to be a part of the mend that fills the void left in the world by his loss.

This is all for you, my son.

Be Kind Like Kaine Book2
Lunch Time

Written By Thomas M. Kaine

Illustrated By Debbie J Hefke

Everyone's favorite time of day was recess.
We'd go out to run and play.

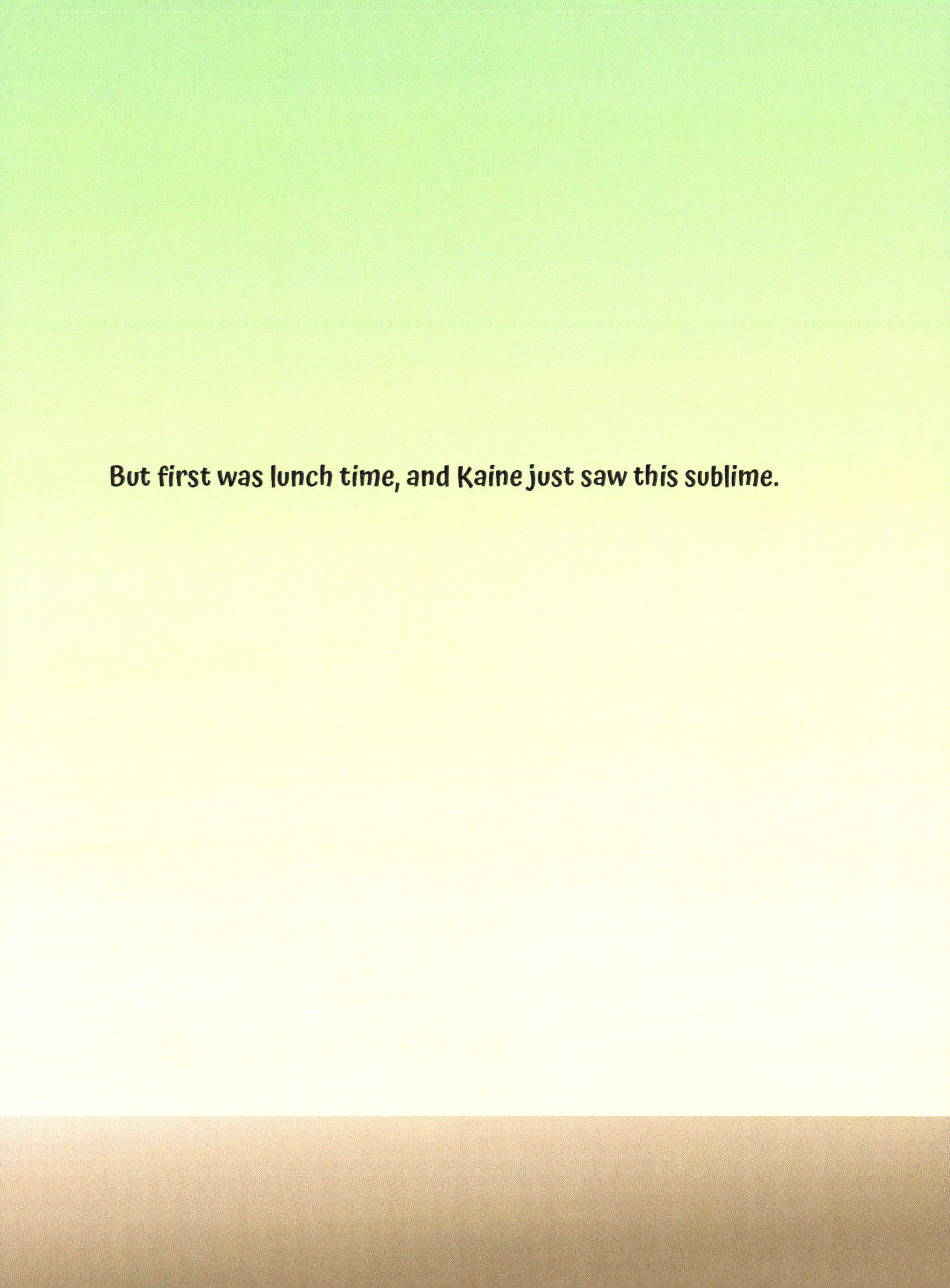

But first was lunch time, and Kaine just saw this sublime.

Yes, food was among his favorite things.
But Kaine would share much better than kings.

His favorite treat in his Bluey tin, was no mere prize for one to win.

For whoever had the least to eat.
They joined Kaine in his feast.

Make no mistake this was no ploy, but simply done to spread the joy.

Even after lunch, Kaine's kindness did not end.

In any situation, if help is needed, Kaine had a hand to lend.

So when you see someone in need, and helping them would show no gain.

Just remember what you learned and how you can.
Be Kind Like Kaine.

Coming Soon Titles

Be kind like kaine on the playround

Be kind like Kaine, last day of school

How to be kind like Kaine